Fracti‹ Decimals Quick Starts

Author: Vicky Shiotsu
Editor: Mary Dieterich
Proofreaders: April Albert and Margaret Brown

COPYRIGHT © 2018 Mark Twain Media, Inc.

ISBN 978-1-62223-698-5

Printing No. CD-405021

Mark Twain Media, Inc., Publishers
Distributed by Carson-Dellosa Publishing LLC

Visit www.carsondellosa.com

Table of Contents

Introduction to the Teacher 1

Fractions

Identifying Fractional Parts 2

Comparing Fractions 3

Fractional Parts of a Number 5

Equivalent Fractions 6

Simplest Form 7

Improper Fractions & Mixed Numbers 9

Using Fractions to Show Division 10

Adding & Subtracting With Like Denominators 11

Least Common Multiple & Greatest Common Factor 13

Adding Fractions With Unlike Denominators 14

Subtracting Fractions With Unlike Denominators 16

Adding Mixed Numbers 17

Subtracting Mixed Numbers 19

Multiplying Fractions 20

Multiplying Mixed Numbers 22

Dividing Fractions 23

Dividing Mixed Numbers 24

Decimals

Tenths & Hundredths 26

Thousandths 27

Decimals & Mixed Numbers 29

Decimals & Place Value 30

Comparing Decimals 32

Comparing Fractions, Mixed Numbers, & Decimals 33

Rounding Decimals 35

Adding & Subtracting Tenths 36

Adding & Subtracting Hundredths 38

Adding & Subtracting Thousandths 39

Multiplying Whole Numbers & Decimals 41

Multiplying Decimals by Decimals 42

Zeros in the Product 44

Dividing Decimals by a Whole Number 46

Writing Remainders as Decimals..47

Dividing Whole Numbers by Decimals 49

Dividing Decimals by Decimals 50

Dividing & Rounding 52

Multiplying by Powers of 10...53

Dividing by Powers of 10 54

Converting Fractions to Decimals...55

Answer Keys...56

Introduction to the Teacher

The short activities presented in *Fractions & Decimals Quick Starts* provide teachers and parents with activities that help students practice and reinforce skills involving fractions and decimals. Used at the beginning of class, quick starts help students focus on topics related to fractions and decimals.

This book has been divided into two sections: the first section focuses on fractions, while the second presents decimals. The skills in each section are presented in a progressive order. Generally, students should master the skills at the beginning of a section in order to successfully complete the activities that are at the end of a section. However, the activities that are presented in any given topic do not need to be presented in a sequential order, since they all relate to the same topic or skill.

Suggestions for use:

- Copy and cut apart the activities that focus on the same topic or skill. Give students one quick start activity each day at the beginning of class.

- Give each student a copy of the entire page to complete day by day. Students can keep the completed pages in a three-ring binder or folder to use as a resource.

- Make transparencies of individual quick starts and complete the activities as a group.

- Provide additional copies of quick starts in your learning center for students to complete when they have a few extra minutes.

- Keep some quick starts on hand to use as fill-ins when the class has a few extra minutes before lunch or dismissal.

 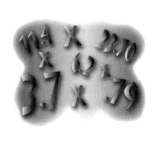 

Fractions

Identifying Fractional Parts 1

Write the fraction for the shaded part.

A.

 _____

B.

 _____

C.

 _____

Identifying Fractional Parts 2

Write the fraction for the shaded part.

A.

 _____

B.

 _____

C.

 _____

Identifying Fractional Parts 3

Write the fraction for each.

A. two-fourths _____

B. three-fifths _____

C. six-tenths _____

D. five-sixths _____

E. four-ninths _____

F. three-thirds _____

Identifying Fractional Parts 4

A. If 5 of 12 flowers are red, what fraction of the flowers are red? _____

B. If 7 of 10 balloons are blue, what fraction of the balloons are not blue? _____

C. There are 9 caps. If 5 caps are white and 2 caps are yellow, what fraction of the caps are white or yellow? _____

Fractions

Identifying Fractional Parts 5

Write two fractions that describe the part of the square that is shaded. Explain your answer.

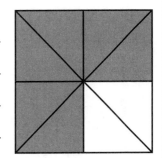

_____

_____

_____

_____

Comparing Fractions 1

Write > or < in the circle to compare the fractions.

A. $\frac{3}{6}$ ◯ $\frac{2}{6}$ B. $\frac{7}{9}$ ◯ $\frac{8}{9}$ C. $\frac{2}{3}$ ◯ $\frac{2}{4}$

D. $\frac{5}{6}$ ◯ $\frac{5}{12}$ E. $\frac{4}{5}$ ◯ $\frac{4}{4}$ F. $\frac{7}{9}$ ◯ $\frac{7}{10}$

Comparing Fractions 2

A. Jim ate $\frac{1}{4}$ of the pizza. Tracy ate $\frac{1}{6}$ of it. Lee ate $\frac{1}{3}$ of the pizza.

Who ate the most pizza? _____

Who ate the least? _____

B. Megan has a container of beads. If $\frac{3}{5}$ of the beads are red and $\frac{3}{6}$ are blue, does Megan have more red beads or blue beads? _____

Fractions

Comparing Fractions 3

Write the fractions in order from the least to the greatest.

A. $\frac{5}{8}$, $\frac{1}{8}$, $\frac{7}{8}$, $\frac{3}{8}$ _____

B. $\frac{1}{7}$, $\frac{1}{2}$, $\frac{1}{3}$, $\frac{1}{9}$ _____

C. $\frac{3}{5}$, $\frac{3}{7}$, $\frac{3}{4}$, $\frac{3}{10}$ _____

D. $\frac{6}{8}$, $\frac{6}{10}$, $\frac{6}{12}$, $\frac{6}{6}$ _____

Comparing Fractions 4

Write >, <, or =. Use the bars to help you.

A. $\frac{1}{2}$ ◯ $\frac{1}{3}$

B. $\frac{2}{6}$ ◯ $\frac{2}{3}$

C. $\frac{3}{6}$ ◯ $\frac{1}{2}$

D. $\frac{3}{4}$ ◯ $\frac{4}{6}$

E. $\frac{1}{2}$ ◯ $\frac{2}{4}$

Comparing Fractions 5

Use the numbers in the circle to fill in the boxes. Write each number only once.

A. $\frac{1}{4} < \dfrac{1}{\boxed{}}$

B. $\frac{2}{6} > \dfrac{2}{\boxed{}}$

C. $\frac{9}{10} > \dfrac{\boxed{}}{\boxed{}}$

Fractions

Fractional Parts of a Number 1

Find the following numbers.

A. $\frac{1}{2}$ of 10 = _____

B. $\frac{1}{3}$ of 15 = _____

C. $\frac{1}{5}$ of 20 = _____

D. $\frac{1}{3}$ of 21 = _____

E. $\frac{1}{7}$ of 14 = _____

F. $\frac{1}{4}$ of 32 = _____

Fractional Parts of a Number 2

A. There were 28 beads. One-fourth of the beads were green. How many beads were green? _____

B. There were 30 students in the class. If one-sixth of them wore glasses, how many students wore glasses? _____

Fractional Parts of a Number 3

How does knowing that $\frac{1}{5}$ of 60 equals 12 help you find out what $\frac{4}{5}$ of 60 equals?

_____

_____

_____

_____

_____

_____

_____

Fractional Parts of a Number 4

Find the following numbers.

A.   What is $\frac{3}{4}$ of 16? _____ $\frac{3}{8}$

B.   What is $\frac{3}{8}$ of 24? _____

C.   What is $\frac{2}{5}$ of 20? _____

D.   What is $\frac{5}{7}$ of 21? _____

Fractions

Fractional Parts of a Number 5

A. Dean baked some cookies. He gave one-half of them to Lee. Now Dean has 18 cookies. How many cookies did Dean bake in all? _____

B. Kwan baked some brownies. Her family ate one-fourth of them. Now there are 12 brownies left. How many brownies did Kwan bake? _____

C. Jamie baked some muffins. She gave half of them to Brent. Then she gave half of what she had left to Sara. Now Jamie has 6 muffins left. How many muffins did Jamie bake? _____

Equivalent Fractions 1

Make equivalent fractions.

A. $\frac{1}{3} = \frac{\Box}{9}$

B. $\frac{3}{5} = \frac{\Box}{10}$

C. $\frac{4}{7} = \frac{\Box}{21}$

D. $\frac{1}{4} = \frac{5}{\Box}$

E. $\frac{2}{5} = \frac{10}{\Box}$

F. $\frac{5}{8} = \frac{20}{\Box}$

Equivalent Fractions 2

Write a fraction for the shaded part. Write two equivalent fractions for each picture.

         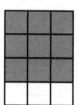

A. _____   B. _____   C. _____   D. _____

Fractions

Equivalent Fractions 3

A. List three equivalent fractions for $\frac{1}{2}$. Look at the numerators and denominators. What pattern do you see? _____

_____

B. List three equivalent fractions for $\frac{1}{5}$. Look at the numerators and denominators. What pattern do you see? _____

_____

Equivalent Fractions 4

Are the fractions in each pair equivalent?

A. $\frac{4}{5}$, $\frac{20}{25}$ _____

B. $\frac{3}{7}$, $\frac{15}{21}$ _____

C. $\frac{2}{3}$, $\frac{14}{24}$ _____

D. $\frac{16}{36}$, $\frac{4}{9}$ _____

E. $\frac{9}{12}$, $\frac{3}{4}$ _____

F. $\frac{15}{25}$, $\frac{4}{5}$ _____

Equivalent Fractions 5

A. A fraction is equivalent to $\frac{1}{2}$. The numerator is a prime number. The denominator is a multiple of 7. What is the fraction? _____

B. A fraction is equivalent to $\frac{5}{7}$. The denominator is 10 more than the numerator. What is the fraction? _____

Simplest Form 1

Is each fraction in simplest form? Write **yes** or **no**.

A. $\frac{3}{8}$ _____

B. $\frac{4}{6}$ _____

C. $\frac{9}{15}$ _____

D. $\frac{5}{12}$ _____

E. $\frac{14}{35}$ _____

F. $\frac{18}{25}$ _____

Fractions

Simplest Form 2

Write each fraction in simplest form.

A. $\frac{6}{10}$ _____

B. $\frac{3}{9}$ _____

C. $\frac{4}{16}$ _____

D. $\frac{3}{15}$ _____

E. $\frac{9}{12}$ _____

F. $\frac{18}{21}$ _____

Simplest Form 3

Circle the fraction in each group that is not in simplest form.

A. $\frac{1}{8}$ $\frac{3}{8}$ $\frac{4}{8}$ $\frac{5}{8}$

B. $\frac{2}{9}$ $\frac{4}{9}$ $\frac{6}{9}$ $\frac{8}{9}$

C. $\frac{3}{10}$ $\frac{5}{10}$ $\frac{7}{10}$ $\frac{9}{10}$

D. $\frac{1}{12}$ $\frac{3}{12}$ $\frac{5}{12}$ $\frac{7}{12}$

E. $\frac{2}{15}$ $\frac{4}{15}$ $\frac{5}{15}$ $\frac{7}{15}$

F. $\frac{3}{18}$ $\frac{5}{18}$ $\frac{7}{18}$ $\frac{11}{18}$

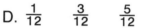

Simplest Form 4

Write the answers in simplest form.

A. There are 20 balloons. Eight balloons are red. What fraction of the balloons is red? _____

B. Janet had $36. She spent $12 on school supplies and $8 on magazines. What fraction of her money did she spend? _____

Simplest Form 5

Write the answers in simplest form.

	Number of Boys	Number of Girls
Room 1	11	13
Room 2	9	15

A. What fraction of the total number of students are boys? _____

B. What fraction of the total number of students are girls? _____

Fractions

Improper Fractions & Mixed Numbers 1

Write a mixed number and an improper fraction that each tells what part is shaded.

A. _____, _____   B. _____, _____   C. _____, _____   D. _____, _____

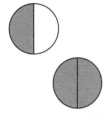

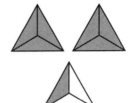
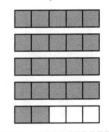

Improper Fractions & Mixed Numbers 2

Write the missing fractions from the number line.

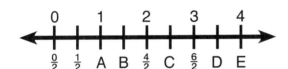

A. _____   B. _____   C. _____   D. _____   E. _____

Improper Fractions & Mixed Numbers 3

A. Lori needs $\frac{1}{2}$ yard of fabric to make a teddy bear. How many

yards of fabric will she need to make 9 teddy bears?

_____

B. Evan needs $\frac{3}{4}$ cup of flour to make 1 batch of brownies. How many cups of

flour does he need to make 5 batches of brownies? _____

Fractions

Improper Fractions & Mixed Numbers 4

Write the mixed numbers as improper fractions.

A. $2\frac{4}{5} =$ _____

B. $3\frac{1}{8} =$ _____

C. $4\frac{7}{10} =$ _____

D. $3\frac{2}{9} =$ _____

E. $2\frac{5}{6} =$ _____

F. $6\frac{3}{5} =$ _____

Improper Fractions & Mixed Numbers 5

Write the improper fractions as mixed numbers or whole numbers.

A. $\frac{15}{2} =$ _____

B. $\frac{9}{3} =$ _____

C. $\frac{18}{7} =$ _____

D. $\frac{25}{6} =$ _____

E. $\frac{29}{8} =$ _____

F. $\frac{20}{4} =$ _____

Using Fractions to Show Division 1

A. Circle the fraction that stands for $10 \div 2$.

$\frac{2}{10}$ $\frac{10}{2}$ $\frac{10}{10}$ $\frac{2}{2}$

B. Circle the fraction that stands for $4\overline{)12}$.

$\frac{12}{4}$ $\frac{4}{12}$ $\frac{4}{4}$ $\frac{12}{12}$

C. Circle the fraction that stands for 8 divided by 5.

$\frac{8}{8}$ $\frac{5}{8}$ $\frac{5}{5}$ $\frac{8}{5}$

Using Fractions to Show Division 2

Divide to change each improper fraction into a whole number.

A. $\frac{12}{6} =$ _____

B. $\frac{15}{3} =$ _____

C. $\frac{16}{4} =$ _____

D. $\frac{20}{2} =$ _____

E. $\frac{18}{6} =$ _____

F. $\frac{24}{3} =$ _____

Fractions

Using Fractions to Show Division 3

Write each division problem as a fraction.

A. $16 \div 8$ _____

B. $14 \div 7$ _____

C. $15 \div 6$ _____

D. $3 \div 9$ _____

E. $4 \div 7$ _____

F. $12 \div 25$ _____

Using Fractions to Show Division 4

Write each division problem in three ways. Use two division symbols and one fraction bar.

A. 21 divided by 9

_____   _____

_____

B. 12 divided by 25

_____   _____

_____

Using Fractions to Show Division 5

Write the answer to each division problem as a mixed number. Use simplest form.

Example: $6\overline{)16} = 2R4 = 2\frac{4}{6} = 2\frac{2}{3}$

A. $3\overline{)20}$ _____

B. $4\overline{)34}$ _____

C. $9\overline{)30}$ _____

D. $8\overline{)50}$ _____

Adding & Subtracting With Like Denominators 1

Add or subtract.

A. $\frac{2}{6} + \frac{3}{6} =$ _____

B. $\frac{7}{9} + \frac{1}{9} =$ _____

C. $\frac{8}{12} + \frac{3}{12} =$ _____

D. $\frac{7}{10} - \frac{4}{10} =$ _____

E. $\frac{10}{20} - \frac{9}{20} =$ _____

F. $\frac{15}{24} - \frac{8}{24} =$ _____

Fractions

Adding & Subtracting With Like Denominators 2

Write the missing numbers.

A. $\dfrac{\Box}{15} + \dfrac{3}{15} = \dfrac{11}{15}$

B. $\dfrac{\Box}{14} - \dfrac{6}{14} = \dfrac{7}{14}$

C. $\dfrac{9}{16} + \dfrac{\Box}{16} = 1$

D. $\dfrac{15}{18} - \dfrac{\Box}{18} = \dfrac{7}{18}$

Adding & Subtracting With Like Denominators 3

Write the missing numbers.

A. $\dfrac{\Box}{10} + \dfrac{3}{10} + \dfrac{3}{10} = \dfrac{\Box}{10} = \dfrac{4}{5}$

B. $\dfrac{7}{18} + \dfrac{\Box}{18} = \dfrac{14}{18} = \dfrac{7}{\Box}$

C. $\dfrac{18}{24} - \dfrac{\Box}{24} - \dfrac{5}{24} = \dfrac{\Box}{24} = \dfrac{1}{3}$

Adding & Subtracting With Like Denominators 4

A. Lisa cut a pizza into 12 equal slices. She ate 2 slices. Mark ate 1 more slice than Lisa. What fraction of the pizza was eaten? _____

B. Kelly bought 1 yard of fabric. She bought $\frac{3}{8}$ yard more fabric than Shannon. How many yards of fabric did Shannon buy? _____

Adding & Subtracting With Like Denominators 5

Write the answers in simplest form.

A. $\frac{2}{6} + \frac{1}{6} =$ _____

B. $\frac{5}{9} + \frac{1}{9} =$ _____

C. $\frac{4}{8} - \frac{2}{8} =$ _____

D. $\frac{11}{12} - \frac{2}{12} =$ _____

E. $\frac{1}{10} + \frac{1}{10} =$ _____

F. $\frac{16}{20} - \frac{10}{20} =$ _____

Fractions

Least Common Multiple & Greatest Common Factor 1

Write the first three multiples of each number.

A. 9 _____, _____, _____

B. 12 _____, _____, _____

C. 15 _____, _____, _____

D. 24 _____, _____, _____

Least Common Multiple & Greatest Common Factor 2

Find the GCF and LCM of each set of numbers.

A. 6, 9, 12   GCF _____   LCM _____

B. 8, 10, 24   GCF _____   LCM _____

C. 12, 30, 18   GCF _____   LCM _____

D. 5, 15, 20   GCF _____   LCM _____

E. 6, 10, 30   GCF _____   LCM _____

Least Common Multiple & Greatest Common Factor 3

A. The GCF of an odd number and an even number is 13. The greater number is 39. What is the lesser number? _____

B. The LCM of two numbers is 24. The GCF is 4. One number is 4 more than the other. What are the numbers? _____

C. The LCM of two numbers is 75. The GCF is 5. The sum of the numbers is 40. What are the numbers? _____

D. The LCM of two numbers is 60. The sum of the numbers is 50. What are the numbers? _____

Fractions

Least Common Multiple & Greatest Common Factor 4

Write the least common multiple (LCM).

A. 8, 12   _____

B. 9, 27   _____

C. 10, 25   _____

D. 12, 18   _____

E. 24, 72   _____

F. 18, 27   _____

Least Common Multiple & Greatest Common Factor 5

Write the greatest common factor (GCF).

A. 18, 27   _____

B. 24, 36   _____

C. 45, 60   _____

D. 25, 75   _____

E. 32, 40   _____

F. 48, 64   _____

Adding Fractions With Unlike Denominators 1

Find the least common denominator for each pair of fractions. Then add the fractions.

A. $\frac{1}{3}, \frac{3}{7}$ _____

B. $\frac{4}{5}, \frac{1}{10}$ _____

C. $\frac{1}{6}, \frac{4}{9}$ _____

D. $\frac{3}{8}, \frac{7}{12}$ _____

Adding Fractions With Unlike Denominators 2

Write each sum in simplest form.

A. $\frac{1}{8} + \frac{1}{4} =$ _____

B. $\frac{4}{10} + \frac{2}{5} =$ _____

C. $\frac{2}{6} + \frac{4}{8} =$ _____

D. $\frac{3}{9} + \frac{1}{2} =$ _____

Fractions

Adding Fractions With Unlike Denominators 3

A. The baker put $\frac{5}{8}$ of the cookies on a tray and $\frac{1}{4}$ of the cookies on a plate. What fraction of the cookies did he put on the tray and plate?

_____

B. Lynn had $\frac{1}{3}$ yard of red ribbon and $\frac{1}{2}$ yard of blue ribbon. How much ribbon did she have in all? _____

Adding Fractions With Unlike Denominators 4

A. Brad bought a pencil for a quarter and an eraser for a dime. What fraction of a dollar did he spend? Write an addition problem with fractions. _____

B. Jenny bought a pen for two quarters and candy for a nickel. What fraction of a dollar did she spend? Write an addition problem with fractions. _____

Adding Fractions With Unlike Denominators 5

Find the least common denominator for each set of fractions. Then add the fractions.

A. $\frac{1}{2}, \frac{3}{8}, \frac{1}{16}$ _____

B. $\frac{1}{4}, \frac{1}{3}, \frac{2}{5}$ _____

C. $\frac{1}{3}, \frac{1}{8}, \frac{1}{10}$ _____

Fractions

Subtracting Fractions With Unlike Denominators 1

Find the least common denominator for each pair of fractions. Then subtract the lesser fraction from the greater one.

A. $\frac{7}{10}, \frac{1}{3}$ _____

B. $\frac{1}{8}, \frac{5}{6}$ _____

C. $\frac{11}{12}, \frac{8}{10}$ _____

Subtracting Fractions With Unlike Denominators 2

Write the answers in simplest form.

A. $\frac{4}{5} - \frac{1}{10} =$ _____

B. $\frac{7}{8} - \frac{2}{5} =$ _____

C. $\frac{5}{6} - \frac{3}{18} =$ _____

D. $\frac{10}{16} - \frac{1}{6} =$ _____

Subtracting Fractions With Unlike Denominators 3

Write the missing fractions.

A. $\frac{4}{5} - \boxed{} = \frac{2}{5}$

B. $\frac{3}{8} - \boxed{} = \frac{1}{4}$

C. $\frac{4}{7} - \boxed{} = \frac{5}{21}$

D. $\frac{2}{3} - \boxed{} = \frac{1}{5}$

Subtracting Fractions With Unlike Denominators 4

Complete the charts.

Subtract $\frac{1}{4}$.	
Input	**Output**
$\frac{7}{8}$	$\frac{5}{8}$
A. $\frac{4}{12}$	
B. $\frac{5}{6}$	

Subtract $\frac{2}{5}$.	
Input	**Output**
C. $\frac{7}{10}$	
D. $\frac{8}{15}$	
E. $\frac{3}{4}$	

Fractions

Subtracting Fractions With Unlike Denominators 5

A. Kris needs $\frac{1}{2}$ cup of sugar and $\frac{3}{4}$ cup of flour. How much more flour does she need than sugar? _____ cup

B. Mike played his guitar for $\frac{2}{3}$ hour on Monday and $\frac{1}{4}$ hour on Tuesday. How much longer did he play on Monday than on Tuesday? _____ hour longer

C. Taylor biked $\frac{4}{5}$ mile on Saturday. That was $\frac{1}{3}$ mile more than he traveled on Friday. How far did Taylor bike on Friday? _____ mile

Adding Mixed Numbers 1

Simplify.   *Example:* $2\frac{7}{5} = 3\frac{2}{5}$

A. $4\frac{5}{3} =$ _____

B. $7\frac{3}{2} =$ _____

C. $6\frac{7}{4} =$ _____

D. $2\frac{8}{2} =$ _____

E. $4\frac{9}{4} =$ _____

F. $3\frac{14}{6} =$ _____

Adding Mixed Numbers 2

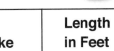

Suppose the snakes on the chart were placed in a line, one behind the other. What would be their combined lengths? Write the answers in simplest form.

A. Fang and Loopy _____

B. Slithers and Sid _____

C. All four snakes _____

Snake	Length in Feet
Fang	$1\frac{1}{2}$
Slithers	$1\frac{3}{8}$
Loopy	$\frac{3}{4}$
Sid	$2\frac{1}{6}$

Fractions

Adding Mixed Numbers 3

Write the sums in simplest form.

A. $1\frac{2}{4}$
  $+ 2\frac{3}{4}$

B. $4\frac{2}{3}$
  $+ 1\frac{1}{3}$

C. $6\frac{4}{6}$
  $+ 3\frac{5}{6}$

D. $2\frac{9}{10}$
  $+ 3\frac{9}{10}$

Adding Mixed Numbers 4

Write the sums in simplest form.

A. $1\frac{6}{8}$
  $+ 3\frac{1}{2}$

B. $2\frac{2}{3}$
  $+ 2\frac{4}{5}$

C. $3\frac{2}{3}$
  $+ 2\frac{5}{9}$

D. $7\frac{3}{4}$
  $+ 4\frac{5}{6}$

Adding Mixed Numbers 5

Write the next three numbers in the pattern.

A. 1, $1\frac{3}{4}$, $2\frac{1}{2}$, _____, _____, _____

B. 2, $2\frac{5}{8}$, $3\frac{1}{4}$, _____, _____, _____

C. $1\frac{3}{5}$, $3\frac{1}{5}$, $4\frac{4}{5}$, _____, _____, _____

Fractions

Subtracting Mixed Numbers 1

Write the answers in simplest form.

A. $4\frac{3}{4}$
$-\ 1\frac{1}{4}$

B. $7\frac{5}{6}$
$-\ 2\frac{5}{6}$

C. $3\frac{11}{12}$
$-\ 3\frac{2}{12}$

D. $6\frac{8}{9}$
$-\ 5\frac{2}{9}$

Subtracting Mixed Numbers 2

Write the answers in simplest form.

A. $5\frac{2}{3}$
$-\ 3\frac{1}{5}$

B. $8\frac{11}{12}$
$-\ 2\frac{3}{4}$

C. $7\frac{7}{8}$
$-\ 3\frac{2}{3}$

D. $9\frac{4}{6}$
$-\ 9\frac{2}{9}$

Subtracting Mixed Numbers 3

Rename the mixed numbers.
Example: $7\frac{1}{4} = 6\frac{5}{4}$

A. $4\frac{1}{3} = 3\boxed{}$

D. $8\frac{5}{12} = 7\boxed{}$

B. $2\frac{5}{8} = 1\boxed{}$

E. $5\frac{9}{10} = 4\boxed{}$

C. $9\frac{3}{4} = 8\boxed{}$

F. $6\frac{13}{15} = 5\boxed{}$

Subtracting Mixed Numbers 4

A. Grant is $3\frac{1}{2}$ inches taller than Kirk. Grant is $56\frac{1}{4}$ inches tall. How tall is Kirk?

_____

B. Ashley is $2\frac{7}{8}$ inches taller than Lee. Lee is $2\frac{5}{16}$ inches taller than Dale. Ashley is $62\frac{3}{4}$ inches tall. How tall is Dale?

_____

Fractions

Subtracting Mixed Numbers 5

Subtract. Regroup first if needed.
Write the answers in simplest form.

$$\textit{Example:} \quad 7\frac{3}{8} = 6\frac{11}{8}$$
$$- 3\frac{5}{8} = 3\frac{5}{8}$$
$$3\frac{6}{8} = 3\frac{3}{4}$$

A. $5\frac{1}{7} =$
  $- 3\frac{2}{7} =$

B. $8\frac{6}{8} =$
  $- 2\frac{2}{3} =$

C. $4\frac{1}{4} =$
  $- 3\frac{3}{5} =$

Multiplying Fractions 1

Cancel to make multiplying easier.

$$\textit{Example:} \quad \frac{2}{5} \times \frac{3}{4} = \frac{\overset{1}{\cancel{2}}}{5} \times \frac{3}{\underset{2}{\cancel{4}}} = \frac{3}{10}$$

A. $\frac{5}{7} \times \frac{3}{5} =$ _____

B. $\frac{3}{4} \times \frac{5}{9} =$ _____

C. $\frac{7}{10} \times \frac{3}{14} =$ _____

D. $\frac{12}{13} \times \frac{13}{36} =$ _____

Fractions

Multiplying Fractions 2

Write each product in simplest form.

A. $\frac{1}{2}$ x 16 = _____

B. $\frac{2}{3}$ x 9 = _____

C. 12 x $\frac{3}{4}$ = _____

D. $\frac{5}{8}$ x 72 = _____

Multiplying Fractions 3

A. What is $\frac{1}{2}$ of $\frac{1}{3}$?

_____

B. What is $\frac{1}{2}$ of $\frac{1}{4}$?

_____

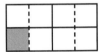

C. What is $\frac{1}{4}$ of $\frac{1}{3}$?

_____

Multiplying Fractions 4

Write each product in simplest form.

A. $\frac{3}{4}$ x $\frac{5}{6}$ = _____

B. $\frac{5}{8}$ x $\frac{1}{5}$ = _____

C. $\frac{4}{10}$ x $\frac{3}{10}$ = _____

D. $\frac{2}{3}$ x $\frac{6}{9}$ = _____

Multiplying Fractions 5

A. One-half of the students in a class are girls. One-fourth of the girls wear glasses. What fraction of the class are girls who wear glasses?

_____

B. Two-thirds of a class play basketball. One-third of the basketball players also play baseball. What fraction of the class plays both basketball and baseball?

_____

Fractions

Multiplying Mixed Numbers 1

Write the products in simplest form.

Example: $4 \times 1\frac{1}{2} = \frac{4}{1} \times \frac{3}{2} = \frac{12}{2} = 6$

A. $3 \times 2\frac{1}{3} =$ _____

B. $2 \times 3\frac{4}{5} =$ _____

C. $\frac{3}{4} \times 2\frac{1}{2} =$ _____

D. $4\frac{1}{8} \times \frac{4}{6} =$ _____

Multiplying Mixed Numbers 2

Write the products in simplest form.

A. $4\frac{1}{6} \times 2\frac{3}{4} =$ _____

B. $5\frac{2}{3} \times 2\frac{1}{4} =$ _____

C. $1\frac{4}{5} \times 1\frac{3}{6} =$ _____

D. $7\frac{1}{2} \times 3\frac{1}{3} =$ _____

Multiplying Mixed Numbers 3

Write >, <, or = to compare the products.

A. $2\frac{1}{3} \times 4\frac{1}{2}$ ◯ $2\frac{1}{7} \times 5\frac{1}{4}$

B. $5\frac{5}{6} \times 3\frac{3}{5}$ ◯ $4\frac{4}{9} \times 4\frac{7}{8}$

C. $2 \times 3\frac{3}{8}$ ◯ $2\frac{7}{10} \times 2\frac{1}{2}$

Multiplying Mixed Numbers 4

A. Lori jogs $2\frac{3}{5}$ miles a day. How many miles will she have jogged after 7 days?

_____

B. If 1 box of cereal fills $15\frac{3}{4}$ bowls, how many bowls will 5 boxes fill?

_____

Fractions

Multiplying Mixed Numbers 5

Write how much you would need of each ingredient to make 3 dozen cream puffs.

A. Water _____

B. Butter _____

C. Salt _____

D. Flour _____

Cream Puffs	
Makes 1 dozen	
Water	$1\frac{1}{2}$ cups
Butter	$\frac{3}{4}$ cup
Salt	$\frac{1}{2}$ teaspoon
Flour	$1\frac{2}{3}$ cups

Dividing Fractions 1

Write the reciprocal of each number.

A. $\frac{1}{3}$ _____

B. $\frac{5}{9}$ _____

C. $\frac{7}{10}$ _____

D. 8 _____

E. $2\frac{1}{2}$ _____

F. $4\frac{5}{6}$ _____

Dividing Fractions 2

Use canceling to help you divide. *Example:* $\frac{2}{5} \div \frac{4}{5} = \frac{2}{5} \times \frac{5}{4} = \frac{\overset{1}{\cancel{2}}}{5} \times \frac{\overset{1}{\cancel{5}}}{\underset{2}{\cancel{4}}} = \frac{1}{2}$

A. $\frac{8}{9} \div \frac{1}{9} = $ _____

B. $\frac{6}{8} \div \frac{3}{4} = $ _____

C. $\frac{4}{7} \div \frac{3}{14} = $ _____

D. $\frac{10}{12} \div \frac{3}{6} = $ _____

Fractions

Dividing Fractions 3

Solve the division problems.

A. $4 \div \frac{1}{4} =$ _____

B. $3 \div \frac{1}{2} =$ _____

C. $6 \div \frac{1}{3} =$ _____

D. $5 \div \frac{1}{10} =$ _____

Dividing Fractions 4

Write a division problem to match the information. Then solve.

A. the quotient of $\frac{2}{3}$ divided by $\frac{1}{2}$

_____

B. the quotient of $\frac{5}{7}$ divided by its reciprocal

_____

C. the quotient of $\frac{3}{4}$ divided by its reciprocal

_____

Dividing Fractions 5

Write the answers in simplest form.

A. $\frac{7}{8} \div \frac{1}{8} =$ _____

B. $\frac{1}{6} \div \frac{3}{2} =$ _____

C. $\frac{5}{3} \div \frac{4}{9} =$ _____

D. $\frac{4}{5} \div 4 =$ _____

Dividing Mixed Numbers 1

Write the answers in simplest form.

A. $\frac{3}{4} \div 3 =$ _____

B. $\frac{4}{7} \div 4 =$ _____

C. $\frac{8}{9} \div 6 =$ _____

D. $\frac{2}{3} \div 3 =$ _____

Fractions

Dividing Mixed Numbers 2

Write the answers in simplest form.

A. $4 \div 1\frac{1}{2} =$ _____

B. $11 \div 2\frac{1}{5} =$ _____

C. $6 \div 3\frac{2}{4} =$ _____

D. $8 \div 2\frac{6}{10} =$ _____

Dividing Mixed Numbers 3

A. Robin had $\frac{5}{8}$ pounds of beads. She put an equal amount into 5 containers. How many pounds of beads were in each container?

_____

B. Mike had a board that was $2\frac{2}{3}$ feet long. He cut it into 4 pieces of equal length. How long was each piece? _____

Dividing Mixed Numbers 4

Write the answers in simplest form.

A. $1\frac{1}{4} \div 1\frac{1}{2} =$ _____

B. $2\frac{4}{5} \div 1\frac{1}{5} =$ _____

C. $6\frac{3}{8} \div 3\frac{1}{4} =$ _____

D. $5\frac{1}{2} \div 2\frac{5}{8} =$ _____

Dividing Mixed Numbers 5

Emma used a recipe that makes three cups of dip. She divided the dip into three containers. How much of each ingredient was in each container?

A. frozen spinach _____

B. onion soup mix _____

C. sour cream _____

Emma's Spinach Dip

$1\frac{1}{2}$ cups frozen spinach

$\frac{1}{2}$ cup onion soup mix

2 cups sour cream

Decimals

Tenths & Hundredths 1

Write a fraction and decimal for each amount.

A. six-tenths _____ _____

B. four-tenths _____ _____

C. one-tenth _____ _____

D. nine-tenths _____ _____

Tenths & Hundredths 2

Write a fraction and decimal for each amount.

A. seventy-six hundredths

_____ _____

B. eighteen-hundredths

_____ _____

C. one-hundredth

_____ _____

D. four-hundredths

_____ _____

Tenths & Hundredths 3

Are the fractions and decimals in each pair equal?

A. $\frac{6}{10}$, 0.6 _____

B. $\frac{27}{100}$, 2.7 _____

C. $\frac{8}{10}$, 0.08 _____

D. $\frac{59}{100}$, 0.59 _____

E. $\frac{1}{10}$, 0.10 _____

F. $\frac{4}{100}$, 0.4 _____

Tenths & Hundredths 4

Circle the number that does not belong in each set.

A. $\frac{5}{10}$ 0.05   0.5

B. 0.76 $\frac{76}{100}$ $\frac{76}{10}$

C. 0.9 $\frac{9}{100}$ 0.90

D. $\frac{3}{100}$ 0.03   0.30

Decimals

Tenths & Hundredths 5

Write two decimals to describe the shaded part for each picture. Use tenths and hundredths.

A. _____   B. _____   C. _____   D. _____

_____   _____   _____   _____

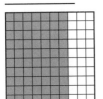 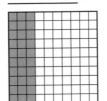   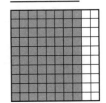

Thousandths 1

Write two decimals that match each value. Use tenths and hundredths.

A. 0.600   B. 0.500   C. 0.900   D. 0.100

_____   _____   _____   _____

_____   _____   _____   _____

Thousandths 2

Write a fraction and decimal for each amount.

A. fifty-four thousandths   _____ _____

B. six hundred eighteen thousandths   _____ _____

C. eight-thousandths   _____ _____

D. nine hundred twenty thousandths   _____ _____

Decimals

Thousandths 3

Write a fraction and a decimal for each amount.

A. 205 thousandths   _____ _____

B. 16 thousandths   _____ _____

C. 899 thousandths   _____ _____

D. 3 thousandths   _____ _____

Thousandths 4

Are the fractions and decimals in each pair equal?

A. $\frac{7}{100}$, 0.007 _____

B. $\frac{5}{1000}$, 0.005 _____

C. $\frac{9}{10}$, 0.009 _____

D. $\frac{20}{100}$, 0.200 _____

E. $\frac{305}{1000}$, 0.35 _____

F. $\frac{80}{100}$, 0.800 _____

Thousandths 5

Circle the number that does not belong in each set.

A. $\frac{2}{100}$ 0.02   0.20

B. $\frac{1}{1000}$ 0.1   0.001

C. $\frac{4}{10}$ 0.400   0.04

D. $\frac{26}{1000}$ 0.26   0.026

Decimals

Decimals & Mixed Numbers 1

Write each mixed number as a decimal.

A. $5\frac{3}{10}$ _____

B. $7\frac{2}{10}$ _____

C. $9\frac{1}{10}$ _____

D. $3\frac{9}{10}$ _____

E. $11\frac{6}{10}$ _____

F. $8\frac{7}{10}$ _____

Decimals & Mixed Numbers 2

Write each mixed number as a decimal.

A. $1\frac{45}{100}$ _____

B. $10\frac{71}{100}$ _____

C. $6\frac{11}{100}$ _____

D. $4\frac{9}{100}$ _____

E. $15\frac{2}{100}$ _____

F. $12\frac{6}{100}$ _____

Decimals & Mixed Numbers 3

Write each decimal as a mixed number.

A. 7.9 _____

B. 6.03 _____

C. 5.37 _____

D. 9.315 _____

E. 4.123 _____

F. 13.009 _____

Decimals & Mixed Numbers 4

Circle the number that does not belong in each set.

A. 3.152 $3\frac{152}{1000}$ $3\frac{15}{100}$

B. $2\frac{7}{10}$ $2\frac{7}{100}$ 2.700

C. $8\frac{9}{1000}$ 8.009   8.09

D. $6\frac{12}{100}$ 6.012 $6\frac{12}{1000}$

Decimals

Decimals & Mixed Numbers 5

Write a mixed number and a decimal to describe the shaded part in each picture.

 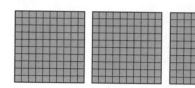

A. _____ , _____   B. _____ , _____

C. _____ , _____

Decimals & Place Value 1

What is the value of the underlined digit? Write **ones**, **tenths**, or **hundredths**.

A. 3.7<u>6</u>   _____

B. 0.<u>4</u>1   _____

C. <u>9</u>.05   _____

D. 2.<u>8</u>0   _____

Decimals & Place Value 2

What is the value of the underlined digit? Write **tens**, **ones**, **tenths**, **hundredths**, or **thousandths**.

A. 59.<u>0</u>73   _____

B. <u>3</u>1.98   _____

C. 6.04<u>2</u>   _____

D. 9.3<u>5</u>8   _____

Decimals

Decimals & Place Value 3

Write the value of the digit 8 in each number.

A. 805.3 _____

B. 329.48 _____

C. 57.86 _____

D. 6.108 _____

Decimals & Place Value 4

Look at the number in the box.

$$402.917$$

A. _____ is in the ones place.

B. _____ is in the hundredths place.

C. _____ is in the tens place.

D. _____ is in the thousandths place.

Decimals & Place Value 5

Write these numbers as decimals.

A. two and three-tenths _____

B. six and nineteen-hundredths _____

C. seventy-eight and eight-hundredths _____

D. ten and five-thousandths _____

E. thirty-seven thousandths _____

F. four and four-thousandths _____

Decimals

Comparing Decimals 1

Write >, <, or = to compare the decimals.

A. 7.6 ◯ 7.1

B. 3.9 ◯ 0.9

C. 4.5 ◯ 4.50

D. 9.01 ◯ 9.1

E. 0.36 ◯ 0.63

F. 5.3 ◯ 5.03

Comparing Decimals 2

A. Which is farther—
2.6 miles or 2.65 miles?

_____

B. Which is longer—
0.5 hour or 0.25 hour?

_____

C. Which weight is heavier—
3.18 pounds or 3.2 pounds?

_____

Comparing Decimals 3

Write >, <, or = to compare the decimals.

A. 2.91 ◯ 2.910

B. 0.05 ◯ 0.005

C. 3.4 ◯ 3.040

D. 8.123 ◯ 8.231

E. 7.5 ◯ 7.501

F. 6.243 ◯ 6.099

Comparing Decimals 4

Write the decimals in each group in order from the least to the greatest.

A. 0.32 _____

0.263 _____

0.163 _____

0.062 _____

B. 0.71 _____

1.7 _____

0.071 _____

0.017 _____

Decimals

Comparing Decimals 5

Write the decimals in each group in order from the least to the greatest.

A. 4.7 _____

    4.3 _____

    4.9 _____

    4.2 _____

B. 2.8 _____

    2.08 _____

    2.83 _____

    2.38 _____

C. 5.6 _____

    5.16 _____

    5.61 _____

    5.06 _____

D. 9.79 _____

    9.97 _____

    9.19 _____

    9.9 _____

Comparing Fractions, Mixed Numbers, and Decimals 1

Circle the number that goes between the two numbers on each number line.

A.
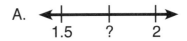

    1.25   1.65

    1.06   2.5

B.
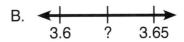

    3.67   3.56

    3.59   3.64

C.
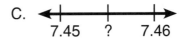

    7.54   7.469

    7.458   7.4

Decimals

Comparing Fractions, Mixed Numbers, & Decimals 2

Write the numbers from the least to the greatest.

A. 1.3 _____

$1\frac{9}{10}$ _____

1.6 _____

$1\frac{4}{10}$ _____

B. $5\frac{6}{100}$ _____

5.6 _____

5.61 _____

$5\frac{16}{100}$ _____

Comparing Fractions, Mixed Numbers, & Decimals 3

A. Circle the number that is between 0.5 and 1.0.

$\frac{7}{100}$ 0.7   1.7

B. Circle the number that is closest to 1.

$\frac{9}{10}$ 0.09   0.99

C. Circle the number that is closest to $\frac{59}{100}$.

0.6   0.95   0.06

Comparing Fractions, Mixed Numbers, & Decimals 4

A. Which number is greater:

$4\frac{1}{2}$ or 4.55? _____

B. Which number is the least:

$\frac{3}{10}, \frac{3}{100}$, or 0.33? _____

C. Which number is the greatest:

$\frac{57}{100}$, 0.7, or 0.577? _____

Comparing Fractions, Mixed Numbers, & Decimals 5

Write the numbers in each group from the least to the greatest.

A. $8\frac{53}{1000}$ _____

8.5 _____

$8\frac{538}{1000}$ _____

8.05 _____

B. $2\frac{268}{1000}$ _____

2.26 _____

$2\frac{8}{10}$ _____

2.608 _____

Decimals

Rounding Decimals 1

Round to the nearest tenth.

A. 0.46 _____

B. 3.72 _____

C. 9.08 _____

D. 6.853 _____

E. 12.84 _____

F. 57.36 _____

Rounding Decimals 2

Round to the nearest hundredth.

A. 0.123 _____

B. 4.049 _____

C. 6.831 _____

D. 0.599 _____

E. 2.573 _____

F. 7.965 _____

0.453.

Rounding Decimals 3

Round to the nearest whole number.

A. 6.4 _____

B. 5.3 _____

C. 0.97 _____

D. 4.37 _____

E. 8.59 _____

F. 1.743 _____

Rounding Decimals 4

A. Which number is 8.3 when rounded to the nearest tenth— 8.36, 8.25, or 8.03?_____

B. Which number is 1.07 when rounded to the nearest hundredth— 1.067, 1.075, or 1.170? _____

C. Which number is 1 when rounded to the nearest whole number— 1.599, 1.8, or 0.73? _____

Decimals

Rounding Decimals 5

A. A tree stands 25.35 feet tall. What is its height to the nearest tenth of a foot?

_____

B. A fence is 9.541 meters wide. What is its width to the nearest meter?

_____

C. A bridge is 0.675 miles long. What is its length to the nearest hundredth of a

mile? _____

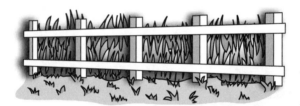

Adding & Subtracting Tenths 1

A. 0.2
  + 0.6
  _____

B. 3.1
  + 4.8
  _____

C. 0.9
  + 0.7
  _____

D. 6.3
  + 0.8
  _____

E. 2.6
  + 9.6
  _____

F. 14.5
  + 35.7
  _____

Adding & Subtracting Tenths 2

A. 0.9
  − 0.6
  _____

B. 8.3
  − 0.3
  _____

C. 2.6
  − 1.4
  _____

D. 18.4
  − 9.8
  _____

E. 21.0
  − 5.9
  _____

F. 46.7
  − 16.8
  _____

Decimals

Adding & Subtracting Tenths 3

Complete the charts below.

Add 0.5	
Input	Output
8.6	9.1
A. 5.5	
B. 11.8	

	Subtract 0.8	
	Input	Output
C.	4.9	
D.	13.6	
E.	27.5	

Adding & Subtracting Tenths 4

Write the next three numbers in each pattern.

A. 1.2, 3.5, 5.8, _____, _____, _____

B. 9.9, 9.0, 8.1, _____, _____, _____

C. 1, 1.6, 2.2, 2.8, _____, _____, _____

Adding & Subtracting Tenths 5

A. How much longer is the purple ribbon than the red ribbon?

_____

B. How much longer is the blue ribbon than the yellow ribbon?

_____

C. What is the total length of all four ribbons?

_____

Length of Ribbon in Centimeters	
Color	Length
Blue	30.2
Red	22.5
Yellow	25.7
Purple	31.4

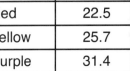

Decimals

Adding & Subtracting Hundredths 1

A. 0.36
  + 0.26

B. 1.43
  + 2.09

C. 9.8
  + 6.24

D. 8.16
  + 2.06

E. 13.99
  + 0.01

F. 25.09
  + 6.27

Adding & Subtracting Hundredths 2

A. 0.85
  − 0.61

B. 4.26
  − 0.95

C. 9.37
  − 2.18

D. 32.01
  − 5.83

E. 14.75
  − 0.87

F. 62.12
  − 15.7

Adding & Subtracting Hundredths 3

A. Keith drove 3.75 miles.

Sherry drove 1.4 miles.

How many miles in total did they drive?

_____ miles

How many more miles did Keith drive than Sherry?

_____ miles

B. A box of crackers weighed 8.5 ounces. A box of cereal weighed 15.25 ounces. How much more did the box of cereal weigh than the box of crackers?

_____ ounces

Decimals

Adding & Subtracting Hundredths 4

A.   6.2
      5.34
  + 8.09

B.   2.8
      2.08
  + 2.88

C.   12.3
      4.56
  + 7.8

Adding & Subtracting Hundredths 5

Write the missing numbers.

A.
$$4\,\square\,.\,\square\,7$$
$$+\quad 3\,.\,6\,\square$$
$$\square\,1\,.\,9\,1$$

B.
$$9\,\square\,.\,3\,1$$
$$-\;\square\,7\,.\,2\,\square$$
$$3\,7\,.\,\square\,5$$

Adding & Subtracting Thousandths 1

A.   0.347
  + 0.062

B.   1.645
  + 2.138

C.   46.952
  + 3.849

D.   82.764
  + 19.328

Adding & Subtracting Thousandths 2

A.   0.697
  − 0.302

B.   1.873
  − 0.048

C.   13.007
  − 2.134

D.   9.761
  − 8.782

Decimals

Adding & Subtracting Thousandths 3

A.   6.19
    − 2.004

B.   8.4
    − 3.691

C.   15.8
    − 9.843

D.   20.06
    − 3.555

Adding & Subtracting Thousandths 4

A. 91.07 + 16.204 = _____

B. 43.8 + 5.903 = _____

C. 50.005 − 3.7 = _____

D. 38.4 − 17.826 = _____

Adding & Subtracting Thousandths 5

A. How much farther did David travel than Yuko?

_____ miles

B. How many miles did Jerry and Maria travel altogether?

_____ miles

C. How many more miles does Yuko need to reach 100 miles?

_____ miles

Distance Traveled in Miles	
Name	**Length of Trip**
Jerry	100.765
Yuko	98.303
David	135.5
Maria	110.68

Decimals

Multiplying Whole Numbers & Decimals 1

Use fractions to multiply. Write the product as a fraction and as a decimal.

Example: $7 \times 0.3 = \frac{7}{1} \times \frac{3}{10} = \frac{21}{10} = 2\frac{1}{10}$ or 2.1

A. 4×0.2 = _____

B. 6×0.4 = _____

C. 9×0.9 = _____

Multiplying Whole Numbers & Decimals 2

A. Kevin jogs 2.6 miles a day. After 7 days, how far will Kevin have jogged?

   _____

B. Carla works 4.5 hours a day. How many hours will she have

   worked after 14 days? _____

Multiplying Whole Numbers & Decimals 3

A. What two numbers have a product of 3.6 and a sum of 3.8? (One number is

   a whole number, and the other is a decimal.)

   _____

B. What decimal and whole number have a product of 4.2 and a sum of 4.4?

   _____

Decimals

Multiplying Whole Numbers & Decimals 4

Multiply.

A. 3 x 0.5 = _____

B. 4 x 0.7 = _____

C. 6 x 0.9 = _____

D. 2 x 2.1 = _____

E. 4 x 1.1 = _____

F. 8 x 3.4 = _____

Multiplying Whole Numbers & Decimals 5

Multiply.

A.   0.43
    x   2
    _____

B.   5.16
    x   7
    _____

C.   1.27
    x   64
    _____

Multiplying Decimals by Decimals 1

Use fractions to multiply. Write the product as a fraction and as a decimal.

Example: $0.7 \times 0.5 = \frac{7}{10} \times \frac{5}{10} = \frac{35}{100}$ or 0.35

A. 0.5 x 0.3 = _____

B. 0.2 x 0.9 = _____

C. 0.8 x 0.6 = _____

D. 0.7 x 0.2 = _____

E. 0.3 x 0.8 = _____

Decimals

Multiplying Decimals by Decimals 2

A.   1.2
   x 0.3

B.   2.4
   x 0.4

C.   9.1
   x 0.5

D.   4.5
   x 0.7

Multiplying Decimals by Decimals 3

A.   0.91
   x 0.3

B.   8.34
   x   0.5

C.   4.23
   x   0.6

D.   1.76
   x   0.9

Multiplying Decimals by Decimals 4

A.   1.3
   x 1.3

B.   2.7
   x 2.3

C.   0.43
   x 3.5

Multiplying Decimals by Decimals 5

A. A muffin recipe uses 0.5 cup of sugar. A cake recipe uses 1.5 times as much sugar. How many cups of sugar does the cake recipe use?

_____

B. Blair's dog weighs 25.8 pounds. Sam's dog is 2.25 times heavier than Blair's dog. How much does Sam's dog weigh?

_____

Decimals

Zeros in the Product 1

Use fractions to multiply. Write the product as a fraction and as a decimal.

Example: $0.3 \times 0.2 = \frac{3}{10} \times \frac{2}{10} = \frac{6}{100}$ or 0.06

A. 0.2 x 0.4 = _____

B. 0.1 x 0.9 = _____

C. 0.4 x 0.04 = _____

D. 0.25 x 0.3 = _____

E. 0.09 x 0.2 = _____

Zeros in the Product 2

A. What number times 0.2 gives a product of 0.06? _____

B. What number times 0.2 gives a product of 0.006? _____

C. What number times 7 gives a product of 0.028? _____

D. What number times 8 gives a product of 0.072? _____

E. What number times 0.9 gives a product of 0.036? _____

F. What number times 4 gives a product of 0.008? _____

Decimals

Zeros in the Product 3

A. 0.2
x 0.2

B. 0.3
x 0.3

C. 0.1
x 0.1

D. 0.02
x 0.6

E. 0.03
x 0.5

F. 0.07
x 0.4

Zeros in the Product 4

A. 0.002
x   7

B. 0.004
x   6

C. 0.008
x   9

D. 0.002
x   2

E. 0.004
x   2

F. 0.009
x   7

Zeros in the Product 5

A. 0.024
x   3

B. 0.013
x   2

C. 0.031
x   3

D. 0.042
x   2

E. 0.061
x   6

F. 0.019
x   5

Decimals

Dividing Decimals by a Whole Number 1

Divide. Then check your answers by multiplying.

$$\begin{array}{r} 0.2 \\ 4\overline{)0.8} \end{array} \rightarrow \begin{array}{r} 0.2 \\ \times\ \ 4 \\ \hline 0.8 \end{array}$$

A. $3\overline{)0.6}$ B. $2\overline{)0.2}$

C. $3\overline{)0.9}$

Dividing Decimals by a Whole Number 2

A. $5\overline{)0.25}$ B. $7\overline{)0.42}$

C. $2\overline{)0.14}$ D. $9\overline{)0.54}$

E. $8\overline{)0.56}$ F. $4\overline{)0.36}$

Dividing Decimals by a Whole Number 3

A. $6\overline{)7.2}$ B. $3\overline{)7.8}$

C. $4\overline{)14.4}$

Dividing Decimals by a Whole Number 4

A. $9\overline{)41.04}$ B. $5\overline{)31.75}$

C. $7\overline{)57.47}$

Decimals

Dividing Decimals by a Whole Number 5

A. Several teams are competing in a relay race. The relay course is 1102.5 yards long. There are 5 runners per team. Each runner will run the same distance. How far will each person run? _____

B. Anna bought 6 yards of fabric for $24.90. What was the cost per yard?

_____

C. Mr. Lang is going to drive 468.81 miles in 3 days. He wants to drive the same distance each day. How many miles will he drive in a day?

_____

Writing Remainders as Decimals 1

Divide. Express the remainders as decimals.

A. $5\overline{)9}$

B. $4\overline{)10}$

```
   1R2              1.4
 5)7    ⟶        5)7.0
 -5                -5
  2                20
                   20
                    0
```

C. $2\overline{)37}$

D. $8\overline{)28}$

Writing Remainders as Decimals 2

A. What was Janet's average score? _____

B. What was Tyler's average score? _____

Janet's Test Scores	Tyler's Test Scores
46	43
45	42
48	45
41	41
47	43

Decimals

Writing Remainders as Decimals 3

Divide. Express the remainders as decimals.

A. $5\overline{)43}$ B. $4\overline{)18}$ C. $8\overline{)58}$

Writing Remainders as Decimals 4

Divide. Express the remainders as decimals.

A. $4\overline{)2.5}$ B. $5\overline{)0.46}$ C. $8\overline{)3.32}$

Writing Remainders as Decimals 5

A. Four textbooks weighed a total of 15.7 pounds. Each textbook weighed the same amount. How much did one textbook weigh?

_____ pounds

B. There were 12 marbles in a bag. The total weight of the marbles was 0.18 pounds. Each marble weighed the same amount. How much did one marble weigh?

_____ pounds

Decimals

Dividing Whole Numbers by Decimals 1

Rewrite the problem to change the divisor to a whole number. Then divide.

   Example: $8 \div 0.2 = 80 \div 2 = 40$

A. $6 \div 0.3 =$ _____   B. $10 \div 0.1 =$ _____

C. $16 \div 0.2 =$ _____   D. $24 \div 0.4 =$ _____

Dividing Whole Numbers by Decimals 2

Change the divisor to a whole number and divide.

A. $0.5 \overline{)25}$ B. $0.7 \overline{)49}$ C. $0.8 \overline{)32}$

Dividing Whole Numbers by Decimals 3

Change the divisor to a whole number and divide.

A. $1.2 \overline{)144}$ B. $2.4 \overline{)48}$ C. $1.7 \overline{)51}$

Decimals

Dividing Whole Numbers by Decimals 4

A. A car travels 2 miles in 2.5 minutes. How far does it travel in 1 minute?

_____

B. A cyclist travels 1 mile in 2.5 minutes. How far does the cyclist travel in 1 minute?

_____

Dividing Whole Numbers by Decimals 5

A. $0.07\overline{)28}$

B. $0.04\overline{)26}$

C. $1.23\overline{)369}$

D. $2.45\overline{)490}$

Dividing Decimals by Decimals 1

Rewrite and divide. $0.3\overline{)1.2}$ → $3\overline{)12}$

$$\begin{array}{r} 4 \\ 3\overline{)12} \\ -12 \\ \hline 0 \end{array}$$

A. $0.4\overline{)2.4}$

B. $0.5\overline{)3.5}$

C. $0.7\overline{)5.6}$

D. $0.8\overline{)14.4}$

Dividing Decimals by Decimals 2

A. $0.05\overline{)6.5}$

B. $0.09\overline{)5.4}$

C. $0.03\overline{)0.21}$

D. $0.08\overline{)0.096}$

Decimals

Dividing Decimals by Decimals 3

A. $0.19\overline{)0.152}$ B. $0.65\overline{)2.08}$ C. $0.25\overline{)4.25}$ D. $0.16\overline{)0.896}$

Dividing Decimals by Decimals 4

A. Jessica collected $12.00 from her mom for the walkathon. Her mom pledged $0.75 for each mile she walked. How far did Jessica walk? _____

B. Mr. Kerns traveled 95.23 miles on 5.35 gallons of gasoline. How many miles did he travel per gallon? _____

Dividing Decimals by Decimals 5

A. 4.2 divided by 0.6 has the same answer as 0.42 divided by what number?

_____

What is the answer? _____

B. 4.2 divided by 0.06 has the same answer as 42 divided by what number?

_____

What is the answer? _____

Decimals

Dividing & Rounding 1

Divide. Then round the answer to the nearest tenth.

A. 8)26   B. 14)85.96   C. 0.4)1.888

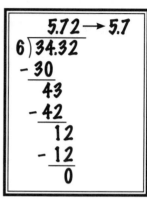

$$
\begin{array}{r}
5.72 \rightarrow 5.7 \\
6\overline{)34.32} \\
-30 \\
\hline
43 \\
-42 \\
\hline
12 \\
-12 \\
\hline
0
\end{array}
$$

Dividing & Rounding 2

Divide. Round the answer to the nearest hundredth.

A. 3)18.402   B. 9)1.674

C. 2)9.91

Dividing & Rounding 3

A. Is the answer to 6.24 ÷ 4 closer to 1.5 or 1.6?

_____

B. Is the answer to 17.41 ÷ 5 closer to 3.48 or 3.49? _____

C. Is the answer to 64.92 ÷ 8 closer to 8.1 or 8.2? _____

Decimals

Multiplying by Powers of 10 1

A. 2.1 x 10 = _____

B. 0.5 x 10 = _____

C. 6.3 x 10 = _____

D. 4.9 x 10 = _____

E. 0.8 x 10 = _____

F. 0.7 x 10 = _____

Multiplying by Powers of 10 2

A. 5.2 x 100 = _____

B. 3.4 x 100 = _____

C. 9.5 x 100 = _____

D. 0.3 x 100 = _____

E. 0.5 x 100 = _____

F. 0.4 x 100 = _____

Multiplying by Powers of 10 3

A. 10 x 0.6 = _____

B. 100 x 0.5 = _____

C. 1,000 x 0.2 = _____

D. To multiply by 10, move the decimal point _____

E. To multiply by 100, move the decimal point _____ _____

F. To multiply by 1,000, move the decimal point _____ _____

Multiplying by Powers of 10 4

A. A cup weighs 0.15 pounds. A bowl weighs 10 times that amount. How much does the bowl weigh?

_____

B. Jim's toy wagon weighs 4.7 pounds. His dad's car weighs 1,000 times that amount. How much does the car weigh? _____

C. A baby kangaroo weighs 1.63 pounds. Its dad weighs 100 times more. How much does its dad weigh?

_____

Decimals

Dividing by Powers of 10 1

A. 0.4 ÷ 10 = _____

B. 0.7 ÷ 10 = _____

C. 3.6 ÷ 10 = _____

D. 2.5 ÷ 10 = _____

E. 12.4 ÷ 10 = _____

F. 19.8 ÷ 10 = _____

Dividing by Powers of 10 2

A. 1.6 ÷ 100 = _____

B. 45.3 ÷ 100 = _____

C. 62.1 ÷ 100 = _____

D. 783 ÷ 100 = _____

E. 265 ÷ 100 = _____

F. 369.2 ÷ 100 = _____

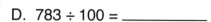

Dividing by Powers of 10 3

A. 56 ÷ 10 = _____

B. 49 ÷ 100 = _____

C. 8 ÷ 1,000 = _____

D. To divide by 10, move the decimal

point _____

E. To divide by 100, move the decimal

point _____

_____

F. To divide by 1,000, move the

decimal point _____

_____

Dividing by Powers of 10 4

Write **>**, **<**, or **=** to compare the quotients.

A. 6.2 ÷ 100 ( ) 62 ÷ 1,000

B. 2.11 ÷ 10 ( ) 211 ÷ 100

C. 54 ÷ 1,000 ( ) 5.4 ÷ 10

Decimals

Converting Fractions to Decimals 1

Change the fractions to tenths or hundredths. Then change them to decimals.

Example: $\frac{3}{5} = \frac{6}{10} = 0.6$

A. $\frac{1}{2}$ = _____

B. $\frac{4}{5}$ = _____

C. $\frac{3}{25}$ = _____

D. $\frac{49}{50}$ = _____

E. $\frac{17}{20}$ = _____

F. $\frac{3}{4}$ = _____

Converting Fractions to Decimals 2

Divide to change the fractions to decimals.

$$\frac{2}{5} = 5\overline{)2.0}$$
$$\begin{array}{r} 0.4 \\ \hline -20 \\ \hline 0 \end{array}$$

A. $\frac{14}{25}$

B. $\frac{1}{8}$

C. $\frac{9}{20}$

Converting Fractions to Decimals 3

Divide to change the fractions to decimals.

A. $\frac{1}{4}$ _____

C. $\frac{2}{8}$ _____

B. $\frac{3}{12}$ _____

D. $\frac{5}{20}$ _____

E. Why do you think you got the results you did? _____

_____

_____

Converting Fractions to Decimals 4

Divide to change the fractions to decimals.

A. $\frac{1}{9}$ _____

B. $\frac{2}{9}$ _____

C. $\frac{3}{9}$ _____

D. $\frac{4}{9}$ _____

E. $\frac{5}{9}$ _____

F. What pattern do you see?

_____

_____

_____

_____

Answer Keys

Fractions

Identifying Fractional Parts 1 (p. 2)
A. $\frac{5}{9}$ B. $\frac{3}{6}$ or $\frac{1}{2}$ C. $\frac{4}{6}$ or $\frac{2}{3}$

Identifying Fractional Parts 2 (p. 2)
A. $\frac{1}{7}$ B. $\frac{7}{12}$ C. $\frac{6}{6}$

Identifying Fractional Parts 3 (p. 2)
A. $\frac{2}{4}$ B. $\frac{3}{5}$ C. $\frac{6}{10}$ D. $\frac{5}{6}$ E. $\frac{4}{9}$ F. $\frac{3}{3}$

Identifying Fractional Parts 4 (p. 2)
A. $\frac{5}{12}$ B. $\frac{3}{10}$ C. $\frac{7}{9}$

Identifying Fractional Parts 5 (p. 3)
$\frac{3}{4}, \frac{6}{8}$
The square can be described as being divided into four equal parts or eight equal parts.

Comparing Fractions 1 (p. 3)
A. >   B. <   C. >   D. >   E. <   F. >

Comparing Fractions 2 (p. 3)
A. Lee; Tracy   B. red beads

Comparing Fractions 3 (p. 4)
A. $\frac{1}{8}, \frac{3}{8}, \frac{5}{8}, \frac{7}{8}$ B. $\frac{1}{9}, \frac{1}{7}, \frac{1}{3}, \frac{1}{2}$
C. $\frac{3}{10}, \frac{3}{7}, \frac{3}{5}, \frac{3}{4}$ D. $\frac{6}{12}, \frac{6}{10}, \frac{6}{8}, \frac{6}{6}$

Comparing Fractions 4 (p. 4)
A. >   B. <   C. =   D. >   E. =

Comparing Fractions 5 (p. 4)
A. $\frac{1}{3}$ B. $\frac{2}{8}$ C. $\frac{4}{5}$

Fractional Parts of a Number 1 (p. 5)
A. 5   B. 5   C. 4   D. 7   E. 2   F. 8

Fractional Parts of a Number 2 (p. 5)
A. 7   B. 5

Fractional Parts of a Number 3 (p. 5)
Four-fifths of 60 is four times more than one-fifth of 60. To find $\frac{4}{5}$ of 60, multiply 12 by 4.

Fractional Parts of a Number 4 (p. 5)
A. 12   B. 9   C. 8   D. 15

Fractional Parts of a Number 5 (p. 6)
A. 36   B. 16   C. 24

Equivalent Fractions 1 (p. 6)
A. $\frac{3}{9}$ B. $\frac{6}{10}$ C. $\frac{12}{21}$ D. $\frac{5}{20}$ E. $\frac{10}{25}$ F. $\frac{20}{32}$

Equivalent Fractions 2 (p. 6)
A. $\frac{1}{2}, \frac{2}{4}$ B. $\frac{2}{6}, \frac{1}{3}$ C. $\frac{1}{3}, \frac{3}{9}$ D. $\frac{3}{4}, \frac{9}{12}$

Equivalent Fractions 3 (p. 7)
A. Examples: $\frac{3}{6}, \frac{4}{8}, \frac{5}{10}$
   Accept reasonable answers. *Example:* The denominator is twice the numerator.
B. Examples: $\frac{2}{10}, \frac{3}{15}, \frac{4}{20}$
   Accept reasonable answers. *Example:* The denominator divided by the numerator equals 5.

Equivalent Fractions 4 (p. 7)
A. yes   B. no   C. no   D. yes
E. yes   F. no

Equivalent Fractions 5 (p. 7)
A. $\frac{7}{14}$ B. $\frac{25}{35}$

Simplest Form 1 (p. 7)
A. yes   B. no   C. no   D. yes
E. no   F. yes

Simplest Form 2 (p. 8)
A. $\frac{3}{5}$ B. $\frac{1}{3}$ C. $\frac{1}{4}$ D. $\frac{1}{5}$ E. $\frac{3}{4}$ F. $\frac{6}{7}$

Simplest Form 3 (p. 8)
A. $\frac{4}{8}$ B. $\frac{6}{9}$ C. $\frac{5}{10}$ D. $\frac{3}{12}$ E. $\frac{5}{15}$ F. $\frac{3}{18}$

Simplest Form 4 (p. 8)
A. $\frac{2}{5}$ B. $\frac{5}{9}$

Simplest Form 5 (p. 8)
A. $\frac{5}{12}$ B. $\frac{7}{12}$

Improper Fractions & Mixed Numbers 1 (p. 9)
A. $1\frac{1}{2}, \frac{3}{2}$ B. $3\frac{3}{4}, \frac{15}{4}$ C. $2\frac{1}{3}, \frac{7}{3}$ D. $4\frac{2}{5}, \frac{22}{5}$

Improper Fractions & Mixed Numbers 2 (p. 9)
A. $\frac{2}{2}$ B. $\frac{3}{2}$ C. $\frac{5}{2}$ D. $\frac{7}{2}$ E. $\frac{8}{2}$

Improper Fractions & Mixed Numbers 3 (p. 9)
A. $\frac{9}{2}$ or $4\frac{1}{2}$ yards   B. $\frac{15}{4}$ or $3\frac{3}{4}$ cups

Improper Fractions & Mixed Numbers 4 (p. 10)

A. $\frac{14}{5}$ B. $\frac{25}{8}$ C. $\frac{47}{10}$ D. $\frac{29}{9}$ E. $\frac{17}{6}$ F. $\frac{33}{5}$

Improper Fractions & Mixed Numbers 5 (p. 10)

A. $7\frac{1}{2}$ B. 3 C. $2\frac{4}{7}$ D. $4\frac{1}{6}$ E. $3\frac{5}{8}$ F. 5

Using Fractions to Show Division 1 (p. 10)

A. $\frac{10}{2}$ B. $\frac{12}{4}$ C. $\frac{8}{5}$

Using Fractions to Show Division 2 (p. 10)

A. 2 B. 5 C. 4 D. 10 E. 3 F. 8

Using Fractions to Show Division 3 (p. 11)

A. $\frac{16}{8}$ B. $\frac{14}{7}$ C. $\frac{15}{6}$ D. $\frac{3}{9}$ E. $\frac{4}{7}$ F. $\frac{12}{25}$

Using Fractions to Show Division 4 (p. 11)

A. $21 \div 9$; $9\overline{)21}$; $\frac{21}{9}$ B. $12 \div 25$; $25\overline{)12}$; $\frac{12}{25}$

Using Fractions to Show Division 5 (p. 11)

A. $6\frac{2}{3}$ B. $8\frac{1}{2}$ C. $3\frac{1}{3}$ D. $6\frac{1}{4}$

Adding & Subtracting With Like Denominators 1 (p. 11)

A. $\frac{5}{6}$ B. $\frac{8}{9}$ C. $\frac{11}{12}$ D. $\frac{3}{10}$ E. $\frac{1}{20}$ F. $\frac{7}{24}$

Adding & Subtracting With Like Denominators 2 (p. 12)

A. $\frac{8}{15}$ B. $\frac{13}{14}$ C. $\frac{7}{16}$ D. $\frac{8}{18}$

Adding & Subtracting With Like Denominators 3 (p. 12)

A. $\frac{2}{10} + \frac{3}{10} + \frac{3}{10} = \frac{8}{10} = \frac{4}{5}$ B. $\frac{7}{18} + \frac{7}{18} = \frac{14}{18} = \frac{7}{9}$

C. $\frac{18}{24} - \frac{5}{24} - \frac{5}{24} = \frac{8}{24} = \frac{1}{3}$

Adding & Subtracting With Like Denominators 4 (p. 12)

A. $\frac{5}{12}$ B. $\frac{5}{8}$ yard

Adding & Subtracting With Like Denominators 5 (p. 12)

A. $\frac{1}{2}$ B. $\frac{2}{3}$ C. $\frac{1}{4}$ D. $\frac{3}{4}$ E. $\frac{1}{5}$ F. $\frac{3}{10}$

Least Common Multiple & Greatest Common Factor 1 (p. 13)

A. 9, 18, 27 B. 12, 24, 36
C. 15, 30, 45 D. 24, 48, 72

Least Common Multiple & Greatest Common Factor 2 (p. 13)

A. GCF–3, LCM–36 B. GCF–2, LCM–120
C. GCF–6, LCM–180 D. GCF–5, LCM–60
E. GCF–2, LCM–30

Least Common Multiple & Greatest Common Factor 3 (p. 13)

A. 26 B. 8, 12 C. 15, 25 D. 20, 30

Least Common Multiple & Greatest Common Factor 4 (p. 14)

A. 24 B. 27 C. 50 D. 36 E. 72 F. 54

Least Common Multiple & Greatest Common Factor 5 (p. 14)

A. 9 B. 12 C. 15 D. 25 E. 8 F. 16

Adding Fractions With Unlike Denominators 1 (p. 14)

A. $\frac{7}{21} + \frac{9}{21} = \frac{16}{21}$ B. $\frac{8}{10} + \frac{1}{10} = \frac{9}{10}$
C. $\frac{3}{18} + \frac{8}{18} = \frac{11}{18}$ D. $\frac{9}{24} + \frac{14}{24} = \frac{23}{24}$

Adding Fractions With Unlike Denominators 2 (p. 14)

A. $\frac{1}{8} + \frac{2}{8} = \frac{3}{8}$ B. $\frac{4}{10} + \frac{4}{10} = \frac{8}{10} = \frac{4}{5}$
C. $\frac{8}{24} + \frac{12}{24} = \frac{20}{24} = \frac{5}{6}$ D. $\frac{6}{18} + \frac{9}{18} = \frac{15}{18} = \frac{5}{6}$

Adding Fractions With Unlike Denominators 3 (p. 15)

A. $\frac{5}{8} + \frac{2}{8} = \frac{7}{8}$ B. $\frac{2}{6} + \frac{3}{6} = \frac{5}{6}$

Adding Fractions With Unlike Denominators 4 (p. 15)

A. $\frac{1}{4} + \frac{1}{10} = \frac{5}{20} + \frac{2}{20} = \frac{7}{20}$
B. $\frac{1}{2} + \frac{1}{20} = \frac{10}{20} + \frac{1}{20} = \frac{11}{20}$

Adding Fractions With Unlike Denominators 5 (p. 15)

A. $\frac{8}{16} + \frac{6}{16} + \frac{1}{16} = \frac{15}{16}$ B. $\frac{15}{60} + \frac{20}{60} + \frac{24}{60} = \frac{59}{60}$
C. $\frac{40}{120} + \frac{15}{120} + \frac{12}{120} = \frac{67}{120}$

Subtracting Fractions With Unlike Denominators 1 (p. 16)

A. $\frac{21}{30} - \frac{10}{30} = \frac{11}{30}$ B. $\frac{20}{24} - \frac{3}{24} = \frac{17}{24}$
C. $\frac{55}{60} - \frac{48}{60} = \frac{7}{60}$

Subtracting Fractions With Unlike Denominators 2 (p. 16)

A. $\frac{8}{10} - \frac{1}{10} = \frac{7}{10}$ B. $\frac{35}{40} - \frac{16}{40} = \frac{19}{40}$
C. $\frac{15}{18} - \frac{3}{18} = \frac{12}{18} = \frac{2}{3}$ D. $\frac{30}{48} - \frac{8}{48} = \frac{22}{48} = \frac{11}{24}$

Subtracting Fractions With Unlike Denominators 3 (p. 16)

A. $\frac{2}{5}$ B. $\frac{1}{8}$ C. $\frac{7}{21}$ D. $\frac{7}{15}$

Subtracting Fractions With Unlike Denominators 4 (p. 16)

A. $\frac{7}{12}$ B. $\frac{7}{12}$ C. $\frac{3}{10}$ D. $\frac{2}{15}$ E. $\frac{7}{20}$

Subtracting Fractions With Unlike Denominators 5 (p. 17)

A. $\frac{1}{4}$ B. $\frac{5}{12}$ C. $\frac{7}{15}$

Adding Mixed Numbers 1 (p. 17)

A. $5\frac{2}{3}$ B. $8\frac{1}{2}$ C. $7\frac{3}{4}$ D. 6   E. $6\frac{1}{4}$ F. $5\frac{1}{3}$

Adding Mixed Numbers 2 (p. 17)

A. $2\frac{1}{4}$ feet   B. $3\frac{13}{24}$ feet   C. $5\frac{19}{24}$ feet

Adding Mixed Numbers 3 (p. 18)

A. $4\frac{1}{4}$ B. 6   C. $10\frac{1}{2}$ D. $6\frac{4}{5}$

Adding Mixed Numbers 4 (p. 18)

A. $5\frac{1}{4}$ B. $5\frac{7}{15}$ C. $6\frac{2}{9}$ D. $12\frac{7}{12}$

Adding Mixed Numbers 5 (p. 18)

A. $3\frac{1}{4}$, 4, $4\frac{3}{4}$ (Add $\frac{3}{4}$ each time.)

B. $3\frac{7}{8}$, $4\frac{1}{2}$, $5\frac{1}{8}$ (Add $\frac{5}{8}$ each time.)

C. $6\frac{2}{5}$, 8, $9\frac{3}{5}$ (Add $1\frac{3}{5}$ each time.)

Subtracting Mixed Numbers 1 (p. 19)

A. $3\frac{1}{2}$ B. 5   C. $\frac{3}{4}$ D. $1\frac{2}{3}$

Subtracting Mixed Numbers 2 (p. 19)

A. $2\frac{7}{15}$ B. $6\frac{1}{6}$ C. $4\frac{5}{24}$ D. $\frac{4}{9}$

Subtracting Mixed Numbers 3 (p. 19)

A. $3\frac{4}{3}$ B. $1\frac{13}{8}$ C. $8\frac{7}{4}$ D. $7\frac{17}{12}$ E. $4\frac{19}{10}$ F. $5\frac{28}{15}$

Subtracting Mixed Numbers 4 (p. 19)

A. $52\frac{3}{4}$ inches   B. $57\frac{9}{16}$ inches

Subtracting Mixed Numbers 5 (p. 20)

A. $1\frac{6}{7}$ B. $6\frac{1}{12}$ C. $\frac{13}{20}$

Multiplying Fractions 1 (p. 20)

A. $\frac{3}{7}$ B. $\frac{5}{12}$ C. $\frac{3}{20}$ D. $\frac{1}{3}$

Multiplying Fractions 2 (p. 21)

A. 8   B. 6   C. 9   D. 45

Multiplying Fractions 3 (p. 21)

A. $\frac{1}{6}$ B. $\frac{1}{8}$ C. $\frac{1}{12}$

Multiplying Fractions 4 (p. 21)

A. $\frac{5}{8}$ B. $\frac{1}{8}$ C. $\frac{3}{25}$ D. $\frac{4}{9}$

Multiplying Fractions 5 (p. 21)

A. $\frac{1}{8}$ B. $\frac{2}{9}$

Multiplying Mixed Numbers 1 (p. 22)

A. 7   B. $7\frac{3}{5}$ C. $1\frac{7}{8}$ D. $2\frac{3}{4}$

Multiplying Mixed Numbers 2 (p. 22)

A. $11\frac{11}{24}$ B. $12\frac{3}{4}$ C. $2\frac{7}{10}$ D. 25

Multiplying Mixed Numbers 3 (p. 22)

A. < ($10\frac{1}{2}$ < $11\frac{1}{4}$)   B. < (21 < $21\frac{2}{3}$)

C. = ($6\frac{3}{4}$ = $6\frac{3}{4}$)

Multiplying Mixed Numbers 4 (p. 22)

A. $18\frac{1}{5}$ B. $78\frac{3}{4}$

Multiplying Mixed Numbers 5 (p. 23)

A. $4\frac{1}{2}$ cups   B. $2\frac{1}{4}$ cups

C. $1\frac{1}{2}$ teaspoon   D. 5 cups

Dividing Fractions 1 (p. 23)

A. 3   B. $\frac{9}{5}$ C. $\frac{10}{7}$ D. $\frac{1}{8}$ E. $\frac{2}{5}$ F. $\frac{6}{29}$

Dividing Fractions 2 (p. 23)

A. 8   B. 1   C. $2\frac{2}{3}$ D. $1\frac{2}{3}$

Dividing Fractions 3 (p. 24)

A. 16   B. 6   C. 18   D. 50

Dividing Fractions 4 (p. 24)

A. $1\frac{1}{3}$ B. $\frac{25}{49}$ C. $\frac{9}{16}$

Dividing Fractions 5 (p. 24)

A. 7   B. $\frac{1}{9}$ C. $3\frac{3}{4}$ D. $\frac{1}{5}$

Dividing Mixed Numbers 1 (p. 24)

A. $\frac{1}{4}$ B. $\frac{1}{7}$ C. $\frac{4}{27}$ D. $\frac{2}{9}$

Dividing Mixed Numbers 2 (p. 25)

A. $2\frac{2}{3}$ B. 5   C. $1\frac{5}{7}$ D. $3\frac{1}{13}$

Dividing Mixed Numbers 3 (p. 25)

A. $\frac{1}{8}$ pound   B. $\frac{2}{3}$ foot

Dividing Mixed Numbers 4 (p. 25)
A. $\frac{5}{6}$ B. $2\frac{1}{3}$ C. $1\frac{25}{26}$ D. $2\frac{2}{21}$

Dividing Mixed Numbers 5 (p. 25)
A. $\frac{1}{2}$ cup   B. $\frac{1}{6}$ cup   C. $\frac{2}{3}$ cup

Decimals

Tenths & Hundredths 1 (p. 26)
A. $\frac{6}{10}$, 0.6   B. $\frac{4}{10}$, 0.4
C. $\frac{1}{10}$, 0.1   D. $\frac{9}{10}$, 0.9

Tenths & Hundredths 2 (p. 26)
A. $\frac{76}{100}$, 0.76   B. $\frac{18}{100}$, 0.18
C. $\frac{1}{100}$, 0.01   D. $\frac{4}{100}$, 0.04

Tenths & Hundredths 3 (p. 26)
A. yes   B. no   C. no   D. yes
E. yes   F. no

Tenths & Hundredths 4 (p. 26)
A. 0.05   B. $\frac{76}{10}$ C. $\frac{9}{100}$ D. 0.30

Tenths & Hundredths 5 (p. 27)
A. 0.7, 0.70   B. 0.3, 0.30
C. 0.1, 0.10   D. 0.8, 0.80

Thousandths 1 (p. 27)
A. 0.6, 0.60   B. 0.5, 0.50
C. 0.9, 0.90   D. 0.1, 0.10

Thousandths 2 (p. 27)
A. $\frac{54}{1000}$; 0.054   B. $\frac{618}{1000}$; 0.618
C. $\frac{8}{1000}$; 0.008   D. $\frac{920}{1000}$; 0.92

Thousandths 3 (p. 28)
A. $\frac{205}{1000}$; 0.205   B. $\frac{16}{1000}$; 0.016
C. $\frac{899}{1000}$; 0.899   D. $\frac{3}{1000}$; 0.003

Thousandths 4 (p. 28)
A. no   B. yes   C. no   D. yes
E. no   F. yes

Thousandths 5 (p. 28)
A. 0.20   B. 0.1   C. 0.04   D. 0.26

Decimals & Mixed Numbers 1 (p. 29)
A. 5.3   B. 7.2   C. 9.1   D. 3.9
E. 11.6   F. 8.7

Decimals & Mixed Numbers 2 (p. 29)
A. 1.45   B. 10.71   C. 6.11   D. 4.09
E. 15.02   F. 12.06

Decimals & Mixed Numbers 3 (p. 29)
A. $7\frac{9}{10}$ B. $6\frac{3}{100}$ C. $5\frac{37}{100}$
D. $9\frac{315}{1000}$ E. $4\frac{123}{1000}$ F. $13\frac{9}{1000}$

Decimals & Mixed Numbers 4 (p. 29)
A. $3\frac{15}{100}$ B. $2\frac{7}{100}$ C. 8.09   D. $6\frac{12}{100}$

Decimals & Mixed Numbers 5 (p. 30)
A. $1\frac{6}{10}$, 1.6   B. $2\frac{73}{100}$, 2.73   C. $3\frac{8}{100}$, 3.08

Decimals & Place Value 1 (p. 30)
A. hundredths   B. tenths
C. ones   D. tenths

Decimals & Place Value 2 (p. 30)
A. tenths   B. tens
C. thousandths   D. hundredths

Decimals & Place Value 3 (p. 31)
A. hundreds   B. hundredths
C. tenths   D. thousandths

Decimals & Place Value 4 (p. 31)
A. 2   B. 1   C. 0   D. 7

Decimals & Place Value 5 (p. 31)
A. 2.3   B. 6.19   C. 78.08
D. 10.005 E. 0.037   F. 4.004

Comparing Decimals 1 (p. 32)
A. >   B. >   C. =   D. <   E. <   F. >

Comparing Decimals 2 (p. 32)
A. 2.65 miles   B. 0.5 hour
C. 3.2 pounds

Comparing Decimals 3 (p. 32)
A. =   B. >   C. >   D. <   E. <   F. >

Comparing Decimals 4 (p. 32)
A. 0.062, 0.163, 0.263, 0.32
B. 0.017, 0.071, 0.71, 1.7

Comparing Decimals 5 (p. 33)
A. 4.2, 4.3, 4.7, 4.9
B. 2.08, 2.38, 2.8, 2.83
C. 5.06, 5.16, 5.6, 5.61
D. 9.19, 9.79, 9.9, 9.97

Comparing Fractions, Mixed Numbers, & Decimals 1 (p. 33)
A. 1.65   B. 3.64   C. 7.458

Comparing Fractions, Mixed Numbers, & Decimals 2 (p. 34)

A. 1.3, $1\frac{4}{10}$, 1.6, $1\frac{9}{10}$

B. $5\frac{6}{100}$, $5\frac{16}{100}$, 5.6, 5.61

Comparing Fractions, Mixed Numbers, & Decimals 3 (p. 34)

A. 0.7   B. 0.99   C. 0.6

Comparing Fractions, Mixed Numbers, & Decimals 4 (p. 34)

A. 4.55   B. $\frac{3}{100}$ C. 0.7

Comparing Fractions, Mixed Numbers, & Decimals 5 (p. 34)

A. 8.05, $8\frac{53}{1000}$, 8.5, $8\frac{538}{1000}$

B. 2.26, $2\frac{268}{1000}$, 2.608, $2\frac{8}{10}$

Rounding Decimals 1 (p. 35)

A. 0.5   B. 3.7   C. 9.1   D. 6.9
E. 12.8   F. 57.4

Rounding Decimals 2 (p. 35)

A. 0.12   B. 4.05   C. 6.83   D. 0.60
E. 2.57   F. 7.97

Rounding Decimals 3 (p. 35)

A. 6   B. 5   C. 1   D. 4   E. 9   F. 2

Rounding Decimals 4 (p. 35)

A. 8.25   B. 1.067   C. 0.73

Rounding Decimals 5 (p. 36)

A. 25.4 feet   B. 10 meters   C. 0.68 mile

Adding & Subtracting Tenths 1 (p. 36)

A. 0.8   B. 7.9   C. 1.6
D. 7.1   E. 12.2   F. 50.2

Adding & Subtracting Tenths 2 (p. 36)

A. 0.3   B. 8.0   C. 1.2
D. 8.6   E. 15.1   F. 29.9

Adding & Subtracting Tenths 3 (p. 37)

A. 6.0   B. 12.3   C. 4.1
D. 12.8   E. 26.7

Adding & Subtracting Tenths 4 (p. 37)

A. 8.1, 10.4, 12.7 (Add 2.3 each time.)
B. 7.2, 6.3, 5.4 (Subtract 0.9 each time.)
C. 3.4, 4.0, 4.6 (Add 0.6 each time.)

Adding & Subtracting Tenths 5 (p. 37)

A. 8.9 centimeters   B. 4.5 centimeters
C. 109.8 centimeters

Adding & Subtracting Hundredths 1 (p. 38)

A. 0.62   B. 3.52   C. 16.04
D. 10.22   E. 14.00   F. 31.36

Adding & Subtracting Hundredths 2 (p. 38)

A. 0.24   B. 3.31   C. 7.19
D. 26.18   E. 13.88   F. 46.42

Adding & Subtracting Hundredths 3 (p. 38)

A. 5.15; 2.35   B. 6.75

Adding & Subtracting Hundredths 4 (p. 39)

A. 19.63   B. 7.76   C. 24.66

Adding & Subtracting Hundredths 5 (p. 39)

A. $\begin{array}{r} 48.27 \\ +\ 3.64 \\ \hline 51.91 \end{array}$ B. $\begin{array}{r} 94.31 \\ -\ 57.26 \\ \hline 37.05 \end{array}$

Adding & Subtracting Thousandths 1 (p. 39)

A. 0.409   B. 3.783   C. 50.801
D. 102.092

Adding & Subtracting Thousandths 2 (p. 39)

A. 0.395   B. 1.825   C. 10.873
D. 0.979

Adding & Subtracting Thousandths 3 (p. 40)

A. 4.186   B. 4.709   C. 5.957
D. 16.505

Adding & Subtracting Thousandths 4 (p. 40)

A. 107.274   B. 49.703   C. 46.305
D. 20.574

Adding & Subtracting Thousandths 5 (p. 40)

A. 37.197   B. 211.445   C. 1.697

Multiplying Whole Numbers & Decimals 1 (p. 41)

A. $\frac{4}{1} \times \frac{2}{10} = \frac{8}{10}$ or 0.8

B. $\frac{6}{1} \times \frac{4}{10} = \frac{24}{10} = 2\frac{4}{10}$ or 2.4

C. $\frac{9}{1} \times \frac{9}{10} = \frac{81}{10} = 8\frac{1}{10}$ or 8.1

Multiplying Whole Numbers & Decimals 2 (p. 41)

A. 18.2 miles   B. 63.0 hours

Multiplying Whole Numbers & Decimals 3 (p. 41)

A. 1.8, 2   B. 3, 1.4

Multiplying Whole Numbers & Decimals 4 (p. 42)

A. 1.5   B. 2.8   C. 5.4   D. 4.2
E. 4.4   F. 27.2

Multiplying Whole Numbers & Decimals 5 (p. 42)
A. 0.86   B. 36.12   C. 81.28

Multiplying Decimals by Decimals 1 (p. 42)
A. $\frac{5}{10} \times \frac{3}{10} = \frac{15}{100}$ or 0.15
B. $\frac{2}{10} \times \frac{9}{10} = \frac{18}{100}$ or 0.18
C. $\frac{8}{10} \times \frac{6}{10} = \frac{48}{100}$ or 0.48
D. $\frac{7}{10} \times \frac{2}{10} = \frac{14}{100}$ or 0.14
E. $\frac{3}{10} \times \frac{8}{10} = \frac{24}{100}$ or 0.24

Multiplying Decimals by Decimals 2 (p. 43)
A. 0.36   B. 0.96   C. 4.55   D. 3.15

Multiplying Decimals by Decimals 3 (p. 43)
A. 0.273   B. 4.17   C. 2.538   D. 1.584

Multiplying Decimals by Decimals 4 (p. 43)
A. 1.69   B. 6.21   C. 1.505

Multiplying Decimals by Decimals 5 (p. 43)
A. 0.75 cup   B. 58.05 pounds

Zeros in the Product 1 (p. 44)
A. $\frac{2}{10} \times \frac{4}{10} = \frac{8}{100}$ or 0.08
B. $\frac{1}{10} \times \frac{9}{10} = \frac{9}{100}$ or 0.09
C. $\frac{4}{10} \times \frac{4}{100} = \frac{16}{1000}$ or 0.016
D. $\frac{25}{100} \times \frac{3}{10} = \frac{75}{1000}$ or 0.075
E. $\frac{9}{100} \times \frac{2}{10} = \frac{18}{1000}$ or 0.018

Zeros in the Product 2 (p. 44)
A. 0.3   B. 0.03   C. 0.004   D. 0.009
E. 0.04   F. 0.002

Zeros in the Product 3 (p. 45)
A. 0.04   B. 0.09   C. 0.01
D. 0.012   E. 0.015   F. 0.028

Zeros in the Product 4 (p. 45)
A. 0.014   B. 0.024   C. 0.072
D. 0.004   E. 0.008   F. 0.063

Zeros in the Product 5 (p. 45)
A. 0.072   B. 0.026   C. 0.093
D. 0.084   E. 0.366   F. 0.095

Dividing Decimals by a Whole Number 1 (p. 46)
A. 0.2   B. 0.1   C. 0.3

Dividing Decimals by a Whole Number 2 (p. 46)
A. 0.05   B. 0.06   C. 0.07
D. 0.06   E. 0.07   F. 0.09

Dividing Decimals by a Whole Number 3 (p. 46)
A. 1.2   B. 2.6   C. 3.6

Dividing Decimals by a Whole Number 4 (p. 46)
A. 4.56   B. 6.35   C. 8.21

Dividing Decimals by a Whole Number 5 (p. 47)
A. 220.5 yards   B. $4.15
C. 156.27 miles

Writing Remainders as Decimals 1 (p. 47)
A. 1.8   B. 2.5   C. 18.5   D. 3.5

Writing Remainders as Decimals 2 (p. 47)
A. 45.4   B. 42.8

Writing Remainders as Decimals 3 (p. 48)
A. 8.6   B. 4.5   C. 7.25

Writing Remainders as Decimals 4 (p. 48)
A. 0.625   B. 0.092   C. 0.415

Writing Remainders as Decimals 5 (p. 48)
A. 3.925   B. 0.015

Dividing Whole Numbers by Decimals 1 (p. 49)
A. $60 \div 3 = 20$ B. $100 \div 1 = 100$
C. $160 \div 2 = 80$ D. $240 \div 4 = 60$

Dividing Whole Numbers by Decimals 2 (p. 49)
A. 50   B. 70   C. 40

Dividing Whole Numbers by Decimals 3 (p. 49)
A. 120   B. 20   C. 30

Dividing Whole Numbers by Decimals 4 (p. 50)
A. 0.8 mile   B. 0.4 mile

Dividing Whole Numbers by Decimals 5 (p. 50)
A. 400   B. 650   C. 300   D. 200

Dividing Decimals by Decimals 1 (p. 50)
A. 6   B. 7   C. 8   D. 18

Dividing Decimals by Decimals 2 (p. 50)
A. 130   B. 60   C. 7   D. 1.2

Dividing Decimals by Decimals 3 (p. 51)
A. 0.8   B. 3.2   C. 17   D. 5.6

Dividing Decimals by Decimals 4 (p. 51)
A. 16 miles   B. 17.8 miles

Dividing Decimals by Decimals 5 (p. 51)
A. 0.06; 7   B. 0.6; 70

Dividing & Rounding 1 (p. 52)
A. 3.3   B. 6.1   C. 4.7

Dividing & Rounding 2 (p. 52)
A. 6.13   B. 0.19   C. 4.96

Dividing & Rounding 3 (p. 52)
A. 1.6   B. 3.48   C. 8.1

Multiplying by Powers of 10 1 (p. 53)
A. 21   B. 5   C. 63
D. 49   E. 8   F. 7

Multiplying by Powers of 10 2 (p. 53)
A. 520   B. 340   C. 950
D. 30   E. 50   F. 40

Multiplying by Powers of 10 3 (p. 53)
A. 6   B. 50   C. 200
D. one place to the right.
E. two places to the right.
F. three places to the right.

Multiplying by Powers of 10 4 (p. 53)
A. 1.5 pounds   B. 4,700 pounds
C. 163 pounds

Dividing by Powers of 10 1 (p. 54)
A. 0.04   B. 0.07   C. 0.36
D. 0.25   E. 1.24   F. 1.98

Dividing by Powers of 10 2 (p. 54)
A. 0.016   B. 0.453   C. 0.621
D. 7.83   E. 2.65   F. 3.692

Dividing by Powers of 10 3 (p. 54)
A. 5.6   B. 0.49   C. 0.008
D. one place to the left.
E. two places to the left.
F. three places to the left.

Dividing by Powers of 10 4 (p. 54)
A. =   B. <   C. <

Converting Fractions to Decimals 1 (p. 55)
A. $\frac{5}{10} = 0.5$ or $\frac{50}{100} = 0.50$
B. $\frac{8}{10} = 0.8$ or $\frac{80}{100} = 0.80$
C. $\frac{12}{100} = 0.12$
D. $\frac{98}{100} = 0.98$
E. $\frac{85}{100} = 0.85$
F. $\frac{75}{100} = 0.75$

Converting Fractions to Decimals 2 (p. 55)
A. 0.56   B. 0.125   C. 0.45

Converting Fractions to Decimals 3 (p. 55)
A. 0.25   B. 0.25   C. 0.25   D. 0.25
All four fractions are equivalent, so their decimal values are the same.

Converting Fractions to Decimals 4 (p. 55)
A. 0.11...   B. 0.22...   C. 0.33...
D. 0.44...   E. 0.55...
F. The numerator becomes the digit for the decimal, and it repeats.